Finding Your Person

even if it's you

HI, HELLO IT'S ANNE
@annnexmp

Finding Your Person

even if it's you

RELATIONSHIP ADVICE FROM TIKTOK'S BIG SISTER

VORACIOUS

Little, Brown and Company
New York   Boston   London

Voracious / Little, Brown and Company
Hachette Book Group
1290 Avenue of the Americas, New York, NY 10104
voraciousbooks.com
First Edition: July 2023

Voracious is an imprint of Little, Brown and Company, a division of Hachette Book Group, Inc. The Voracious name and logo are trademarks of Hachette Book Group, Inc.

The publisher is not responsible for websites (or their content) that are not owned by the publisher.

The Hachette Speakers Bureau provides a wide range of authors for speaking events. To find out more, go to hachettespeakersbureau.com or email HachetteSpeakers@hbgusa.com.

Little, Brown and Company books may be purchased in bulk for business, educational, or promotional use. For information, please contact your local bookseller or the Hachette Book Group Special Markets Department at special.markets@hbgusa.com.

Illustration credits appear on p. 192.

Produced by Indelible Editions

INDELIBLE
EDITIONS

ISBN 9780316522359
LCCN 2022950657

Printing 1, 2023

LSC-C

Printed in the United States of America

Contents

Hi, hello it's Anne

How did I end up writing a book? It's a funny story. When I was growing up, my friends and family always came to me for advice. As the eldest daughter in my Filipino American family, I provided guidance to others, hoping somehow to be the big sister I never had. This evolved over time into posting advice videos for friends on TikTok.

For years, it was always "service above self" for me, putting everything and everyone before my own needs. At the time, it felt right . . . perfect, even. In retrospect, I spent so much time giving love to everyone else that I didn't have any left for myself. While I don't regret it, I just wish I had learned to love myself the way I loved everyone else.

Finding Your Person (Even If It's You) is everything I've learned from all types of relationships—romantic, platonic, and the relationship I have with myself—both in real life and through interacting with my wonderful supporters on TikTok. Like a hug in book form, I want to help make the tough times a little easier and your bonds a little stronger.

ROMANTIC
ROMANTIC
ROMANTIC
ROMANTIC

Relationships

While love can be beautiful, it can also be scary, messy, unpredictable, and heartbreaking. Opening up to someone emotionally can be a transformative process, so let's make sure it changes your life for the good!

Come with intention and avoid awkwardness by asking a question.

Acknowledge their vibe. If they're happy, be like, "Hey, sup?" If they look sad or frustrated, ask, "Hey, are you okay?"

Saying "Hi" When You Like Someone

When you leave, do it with a compliment or affirmation, even if it's just "Great to see you."

If they are too far away or with a group, just catch their eye, nod your head, smile, and then slowly look away.

When you first like someone

It's weird, right? Maybe your first crush was an actor or musician, which was easy because they didn't even know you existed. Then one day, you meet someone and realize your heart is beating faster than it does at the gym. Suddenly, you're looking for this person everywhere you go.

You awkwardly make eye contact, and you don't know if you should smile, wave, or just act like you were spacing out. You're disappointed when they aren't around, and you're happy when they are. Yet you can't say one word to them without overthinking the whole conversation afterward (if you can say one word to them at all).

While liking someone can feel monumental, try to put it into perspective. Keep in mind that they are just one of many amazing people you'll like in your life. They're each going to be special in their own way, and some will make your life better, and others, I'm sorry to say, will disappoint you. But each one is going to change you in some way.

Remember: you will always grow through what you go through.

Are you ready for a relationship?

Are you prepared to trust your heart to someone else? And beyond protecting your own heart, are you willing to be responsible for someone else's? These are the questions you need to ask yourself before entering into a relationship.

Film and television have led us to think that finding a partner is the magic fix-it fairy tale that will complete us or solve all our problems.

The truth is, even the most effortless connections take work to maintain. A relationship requires you to be selfless and is filled with compromise. You must consider someone else's needs and be willing to emotionally support them.

Even if you're swept away, it can also help to be honest with yourself that while this may be your first relationship, it probably won't be your last.

It might just be a stepping stone to understanding your own romantic desires.

EASY WAYS TO SHOW
you care

1

2

3

If they mention a song they like, play it the next time you are together.

Ask to take a photo with them when you are enjoying a moment, and then send it to them later.

Ask about their well-being— have they had anything to eat today? Are they tired?

What if we forget the doubt and just pursue it?

What if, for once, we ignore our heads and stop overthinking the consequences and just allow ourselves to feel? What if we agree to break down our walls and simply enjoy each other's company? Will I hurt you? Maybe. Will you hurt me? Probably. But maybe I'll know what it's like to laugh with you. I'll understand how it feels to hold you. I'll get to know you inside and out. Maybe I'll regret nothing.

I want this narrative in my head to become a reality and not remain some made-up tale of what could have been. I'd rather have you completely for a couple of chapters and let my feelings bleed through the pages.

Because whether you cry happy tears or sad ones at the end of the story, it will still be beautiful . . . because you were in it.

Signs you are
head over heels

- The minute they walk into a room, you get an instant serotonin boost.

- You keep your notifications on when your phone is normally on silent mode, so you don't miss anything.

- How they feel on the daily affects your mood as well.

- You don't see any flaws in them, even if your friends see red flags.

- They are the last person you think about before you go to sleep, which either brings you joy or causes you pain, depending on the day.

- Every mention of love, whether in songs or videos, brings them to mind.

3 signs that you two are eventually going to date

1. You are extremely protective of them. You might say, "They're my best friend and I don't want them hurt." But every time they end up dating someone else or talking to someone else, why do you get a little jealous? Why do you never approve of that other person?

2. You two have these vulnerable moments with each other where you think, "Wow, I don't think I've ever been this open with anyone else."

3. Everyone around you kinda just sees it. You can say that they are like a brother or sister to you, but your friends are sure it is something more—that is the biggest tell.

The talking stage

I'm not sure what we are—are we friends? More than friends? Only going to be friends? Or are we just killing time until you find someone you actually like? Maybe I'm just here to keep you company. I'm not sure what to think.

What I do know is that I like you.

I like the way you ask how my day was. How when you call, my heart jumps at the sound of your voice. I like it all. So maybe I'm reading a little too much into it. Maybe there's nothing real between us. But I'm going to be here 'til we figure that out, *if* we figure it out.

I'm not sure
what we are,
but I'm more
than sure we
could be amazing.

Using your eyes

TO GET YOUR CRUSH'S ATTENTION

1 When your crush is talking, maintain eye contact but also raise your eyebrow just slightly to show that you're very interested in what they're saying.

2 When you catch their eye from across the room, be sure to smile, even if it's just with your eyes.

3 If you ask them for any kind of favor, use the puppy dog eyes, because I promise you they cannot say no to the puppy dog eyes (basically making intense eye contact and giving a hopeful look). And then you add the eyebrow lift—come on!

Turning someone down with kindness

Do you know what's worse than saying no to someone? It's saying yes to spare their feelings or to avoid feeling awkward. Plus, it's just cruel to give them false hope. Here are a few tips on how to turn someone down as nicely as you can:

- Acknowledge their interest in you.

- Appreciate the effort it took for them to ask you out.

- Tell them the truth, whether it's just not the right time for you or you don't think of them in that way.

- Don't talk about it to anyone you know who might mock them or spread word about the rejection.

- Don't act weird or avoid them when you see them afterward.

BODY LANGUAGE

that shows they like you

- The second they see you, their eyes get wider.

- When you're in a group of people, you two tend to make eye contact randomly.

- This one's really important: they lean in toward you when you're talking, like they're trying to get into your little bubble of personal space.

- If they notice that you're actually listening to them, they nervously continue to talk about random things to keep your attention.

If you really like someone, you don't forget to text back.

The ghost of you

Has this ever happened—you two were texting each other back and forth, it felt like a relationship was forming, and then all of sudden they stopped? The conversations dry up and you start to question yourself, like, **What did I do wrong? Am I not that interesting?** Maybe you get really sad about it.

After you've finally let it go, you get another text message from them like a week later, "I'm so sorry I was so busy. I didn't mean to not reply." So you forgive them, and it's fine. But then all of sudden the texts go dry, and you're just like, "What, this again?" And then you start to question your worth all over again. But let me stop you here.

It doesn't take days to be like, "Oh, I'm sorry, I was busy." If you like someone, chances are you say something like, "Hey, I'm busy, but let me catch up with you later." The same goes for them. It's not that confusing or hard to do.

Don't put yourself through it again— walk away.

Subtle ways to find out if they like you

HERE ARE SOME CLUES:

Ask them their celebrity crush—if the celeb in question looks like you, you're probably their type.

They remember what you mention and give you small gifts—like if you say you love Flamin' Hot Cheetos, they randomly buy you some.

If they accidentally offend you, they apologize all over themselves.

Record a video with them. When you rewatch it, see if they look at you while you're not looking at them. The eyes tell it all.

They notice and compliment you when you wear something new or try a new hairstyle.

Ask them to pick between two photos of you for a post. If they don't give it any thought and just kind of pick one, they're probably not interested. But if they're a little more specific, like "this one's nice because your smile looks real," they might secretly like you.

They might unconsciously mimic your gestures. For example, if you cross your arms, and they cross their arms right after, that shows they are paying attention to you.

Online dating yellow flags

Online dating takes courage—you are putting yourself out there and admitting you want to find love. But you should also be careful. **Trust takes time.** Here are a few things to keep in mind on the sites:

- Make sure they have a profile picture and multiple other pictures on their account. Also don't meet until they've told you both their first and last name and you've done an internet search to see that their photos match their name. Better safe than sorry.

- If it's the first date, share your location with a close friend using an app.

- Meet them in public and let someone else know where and when you're meeting. Please make sure there are plenty of people around.

- Be wary if they start opening up to you way too fast or make you uncomfortable with too many personal questions.

- Never give them your number or tell them specifically where you are from until after you've met a few times in person. To continue talking to them, just message through other social media apps.

- Listen to your intuition.

If it feels weird, walk away and tell your friends your location so they are aware.

5 WAYS TO
flirt with them

1
While it can be nerve-wracking, maintain eye contact.

2
Be a little bold—if appropriate, occasionally touch their arm.

3
Use their name in conversation—people love that.

4
This one's obvious, but tease them a little bit and try to develop some inside jokes.

5
Oddly specific, but it works: When you leave, give them the once over, then walk away. Turn back for one more smile, then keep walking.

Compliments she might give if she likes you

She may be into you if:

- She says you smell nice.

- She tells you that you have a really nice smile or a great laugh.

- She enjoys talking to you.

- She compliments you on who you are as a person versus physical appearance.

- She delivers the top-tier compliment: you make her happy.

Early stage red flags

- They just got out of a long relationship. Sure, they may be interested in you, but they might also be using you as a distraction from their current heartbreak.

- They love-bomb you, showering you with attention until they've got you hooked, and then it just dries up. This kind of person might just love the pursuit.

- They insist on knowing exactly why you aren't in a great mood, even if you don't want to talk about it. This behavior reveals a level of insecurity that might later turn into possessiveness or jealousy.

- They constantly forget to text you back or to message you back or to call you back. Other than someone who's crazy tired, who forgets to respond to somebody they're really interested in? No one.

- They're too quick to say, "I love you." If it is early days, they might be projecting, loving the **idea** of you.

- They bring up their ex way too much. Even if what they're saying is supposed to come off as a compliment to you—no, no, no, no. They aren't over their ex yet.

When you like someone who doesn't like you

While it's not the end of the world, it can hurt like it is when someone doesn't reciprocate your feelings—I get that. You have invested time getting to know this person, prioritized them, and gone on an emotional roller coaster every time they came around. But it doesn't matter because, in the end, they didn't feel the same.

One thing you should know is that their inability to see your worth, to see your potential, and to fall for your personality does not devalue you as a person.

Just because this one person:

- doesn't like you, that doesn't mean someone else won't.

- thinks you're not their type, that doesn't mean you aren't someone else's.

- didn't want to take a chance on you, that doesn't mean someone else won't. One day, you are going to be so happy this one person didn't want you because you'll be so happy with someone else.

One day, someone is going to be so thankful you are theirs. Trust the process.

The universe works in mysterious ways. It will break you in order to prepare you for what's truly meant for you.

Believe that.

Early stage green flags —————

- They ask questions to get to know you and reciprocate the energy by answering your questions as well.

- They introduce you when they randomly bump into their friends in public.

- They find it important to reply to messages and answer your phone calls, and communicate in advance when they will be busy, and apologize if their responses aren't as interesting or fast.

- They are never late to see you.

- They want to take their time getting to know you rather than speeding through the talking stage.

- They communicate respectfully when they are bothered by something you said or did.

- They schedule plans with you in advance to ensure seeing you.

- Their friends are aware you exist.

- You two enjoy each other's company effortlessly.

Signs their best friend likes you
(BUT THEY DO TOO)

They're supposed to be a wingman for their friend but they still hang around you when their friend isn't there.

When it's just you and them, the energy is different, and you're vibing in a good way. But when their friend arrives, they're suddenly standoffish, because they're trying to let their friend have the spotlight.

They always hype up their best friend but they have your back. If their best friend shows any signs of possibly hurting you, they say something.

By the way, if you are that unlucky person allowing your best friend to pursue the person you like—cheers to you. You're a really good person, but I know that it has got to hurt you.

Falling for your best friend

Was this intentional? Maybe not, but let's be honest—they're your best friend for a reason, right? Maybe you weren't attracted to them in the beginning, and then they did that thing where they made you feel safe and they were always there to listen on your good and bad days. You find yourself excited to tell them every little thing. Maybe your family likes them just as much as you do.

Everything was fine until one day you stared at them a little too long and you realized you have fallen. Which completely ruins everything, because now they've started to notice that you get all weird around them. Your heart wants to tell them, but your head tells you to shut up. You just want to confess your feelings, have them say, "I love you too," and live **happily ever after.**

You aren't going to tell them, though, right? You think it's safer to hold on to the friendship than to potentially ruin it. Why? Because while relationships come and go, friendships can last a lifetime. **Are you okay with that, though?** Truly? You don't mind watching your best friend fall for someone else? It won't bother you to hang out with their new significant other? Or that the new significant other will end up being the person your best friend runs to for advice, comfort, and love? Doesn't the thought of all this break your heart?

Here's what I think you should do: tell them. Sort out your emotions, and after you do, if this person is worth it to you, tell them. Life is too short to wonder about the what-ifs, maybes, and hopefullys. If they really are your best friend, you two will be okay even if they don't feel the same way. If they do feel the same way (fingers crossed), you're welcome— I expect an invite to the wedding. But in all seriousness, you never know until you try.

Quit playing defense and shoot your shot.

How to tell if she likes you: the hoodie method

If a girl is cold and you offer her your hoodie and she says no, she's not interested. But if she says yes, there's a chance she's interested.

If she gives back your hoodie at the end of the night, it shows that she just appreciated the gesture but she's most likely thinking of you as a friend. But if she takes it home with her, she might like you.

If she takes your hoodie home, washes it, and then gives it back to you the next time she sees you, she's a nice person but might not be all that interested.

However, if she takes your hoodie home, jokes that she wears it constantly, and teases you about how you're never gonna get your hoodie back, she definitely likes you.

Love out of my comfort zone

I enjoy my routines. I like knowing what's coming, and what I'm going to be doing every day. Surprises can give me anxiety. Uncertainty makes me uncomfortable. **Then you came along.**

When I first met you, I didn't think much of it. A quick "hi, hello" and a simple "take care, hope to see you again" turned into daily good mornings and good nights. You broke my routine. I don't know what is going to happen next. Will you like me next week the way you do right now? Who knows. Maybe you won't, but I'm going to stick around and find out.

You taught me that there is beauty in not knowing everything. You taught me that there can be a kind of peace in uncontrollable situations. I used to enjoy my routines. Now I might not know what's coming next, but one thing I'm certain of is . . .

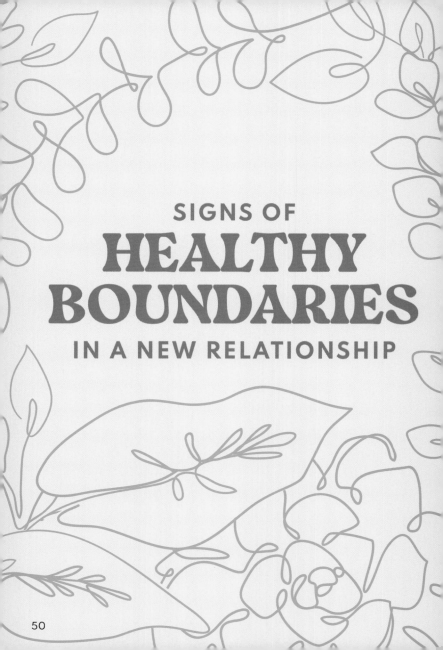

SIGNS OF
HEALTHY
BOUNDARIES
IN A NEW RELATIONSHIP

They are good for you when they:

- Encourage you to spend time alone with your friends.

- Respect your responsibilities and schedule.

- Don't push you to go places that make you uncomfortable.

- Don't get jealous when you talk with other people.

- Understand that you'll talk about things when you are ready.

- Don't look through your phone.

- Don't insist you hang out with people you really don't like.

- Respect your opinions, even if they don't agree.

I knew I was in love when . . .

I knew I was in love when someone was flirting with me, but it didn't matter because it wasn't you. I knew I was in love when I was no longer hesitant about commitment. I knew I was in love when you jokingly brought up children in the far future and it didn't scare me off. I knew I was in love when you saw my blank expression as a silent cry for help and talked me through a panic attack. I knew I was in love when I was given this opportunity to speak on love, and **all I thought about was you.**

8 small ways to strengthen your relationship

1. Have a date at least once a week, even if it is just coffee.

2. Understand that you don't need each other, you want each other, and that's a choice you make every day.

3. Communicate when you're busy.

4. Reassure each other randomly that you care for and miss each other.

5. Comment on the small things that make them special.

6. Send good morning and good night texts.

7. Try new things together.

8. Realize that you do not complete each other, you only complement each other as individuals.

Afraid it's too good to be true

Have you ever met someone and thought, *Wow, this person is unreal*. You two click, you vibe so well it's almost magical. It's almost . . . too good to be true? Whether romantically or platonically, this can be beautiful and terrifying at the same time. Why?

Because for the first time you are afraid to lose someone.

So maybe you don't realize it, but you push them away. You start talking to them less. You dodge their hangouts. You let the phone hit voice mail. You detach yourself almost completely. All of a sudden, **you two are nearly strangers again.**

Let me ask, did they do any harm to your energy? Did they cause you to feel insecure about the relationship or friendship? Did they actually do anything wrong? No? Wonderful. You're not going to want to hear this, but I'm going to say it anyway: you lost. You lost someone who saw your worth, who tried to be there for you, someone who

willingly and voluntarily put forth the effort because
they believed you deserved it.

I understand wanting to run before things take a
turn for the worse, but **quit trying to control
the story.**

Give this person the opportunity to prove you wrong.
Trust until they give you a reason not to. The truth?
Everyone is going to hurt you somehow, sometime.

**You just have to decide who's worth the
heartache.**

1

When you come around, she starts playing with her hair, usually because of nerves.

2

Yes, we ladies put on makeup and look cute just for ourselves—don't get that twisted. But if she's interested in someone, you will never catch her slippin'. She always looks good.

10 things girls do when they like you...

3

Not only will she message you throughout the day, but she will make it very clear that she has paid attention. She'll be out here trying to impress you by remembering little things you said in passing.

4

She'll start hugging you hello, where she might not have before.

5

If you see her at a party alone, she'll pick up her phone and immediately start texting, probably to her friends to let them know you are there.

6

She starts saying things that you say, doing things that you do, and listening to your music.

7

She won't be able to maintain eye contact.

...that you might not notice

She'll playfully tell you you're annoying and jokingly be like, "I hate you."

8

She will match your timeline on messages so she doesn't appear too eager. So if it takes you two minutes to reply to her, it's gonna take her two minutes to reply to you.

9

She's gonna make her way into your daily routine, some way, somehow.

10

Being so in love you're scared

Why am I having trouble believing that you actually want to talk things out when we're upset with each other? That you know just how to reassure me when I get insecure (which is often)? You think my quirks are cute? You do nice things randomly, like buy me flowers? You're happy to go on night drives with me when I can't sleep?

Before I met you, I felt like having all those things was impossible. I didn't think I deserved to be treated so well. I'm not feeling sorry for myself— **I've never had anyone try so much for me.**

It's different, but I think I could get used to it.

What's your love language?

Understanding the way you love and want to be loved is important when you are getting close to someone new. For example, I adore quality hangouts. If I were dating someone who enjoyed giving gifts, while I appreciate that, it would not make me as happy as just spending time together. In his bestselling book *The Five Love Languages*, Gary Chapman defines the way you give and receive affection as your love language.

We tend to be so wrapped up in our own love language that we often fail to remember that **everyone loves differently**. So for you, affection could be expressed through hugs and kisses, while for someone else it may be frequently texting compliments or "I love you." Or maybe your partner is not physically affectionate but instead constantly does small things that make your life easier, like filling your gas tank or packing your lunch. As a new couple, you have to give it some time before you figure out each other's love language.

Relationship dos and don'ts

Do: practice open communication and comprehension. Communication is important, but it's pointless if you refuse to understand the other person's point of view.

Don't: try to control their opinions. Agree to disagree if the issue is too difficult to ignore. Later, you can either talk about the topic or, if it is a deal-breaker, walk away.

Do: remember to make them feel special. It can be something big, like taking them out to their favorite restaurant, or small, like leaving a note in their coat pocket.

Don't: let your insecurities make you assume the worst.

Do: let them know when you are busy that you can make time for them later.

Don't: make promises you can't keep.

Do: text them good morning and good night.

Don't: use their past as ammo for future arguments.

Do: voice your opinions, but also find compromises.

Don't: ignore them when you're upset.

Do reassure your
partner of your feelings
for them whenever
you can.

Don't say
"I love you" if
you don't mean it.

7 things guys do when they like you...

1

When you two are talking with each other, his phone is nowhere to be found.

2

You think it's coincidental that you see him everywhere, but no, that's on purpose—he likes being around you.

He'll text and call you all the time but play it off, saying, "Oh, I'm bored, I have nothing else to do, so might as well talk to you." Such a lie.

3

4

If he's taking a while to respond to your texts, chances are that it's because he just doesn't know what to say, but he wants to write something that you can respond to.

He'll start calling you his best friend. You probably don't even know each other that well, but all of a sudden you're his best friend? Stop that—just say you like me already.

5

6

When you are teasing each other back and forth, you might say something that lands. He will kinda take a little step back, look you up and down, and nod and smile. It's like a nod of approval— he's impressed.

7

When you are walking together, he'll match your stride and turn his body to you. Sure, he might bump into what's in front of him, but you'll be beside him, so he'll take the risk.

... that you might not notice

I was your one time

How did this happen? I had imagined every possible scenario with you, but somehow this one didn't cross my mind. One day, we were as close as we could physically be, and then you woke up the next day acting as if I never existed. You explored my world, and then never spoke to me again. It broke me a little to realize you weren't interested in me as a person. That you didn't even like me.

Now I'm stuck here pretending like I'm okay.

But I'm not. You knew I wanted something real, but that didn't stop you from taking what you wanted and leaving. You probably won't think about it again, but I will. From now on, I'll doubt the quick rush to affection, the rush to trust. My time with you has taught me to stop and think. For me, you've come to define the term *red flag*.

If they loved you, you would feel loved.

You make me want to believe

Your smile is so contagious that I can't stay sad, even if I try. You constantly tell me I'm beautiful, but the joke's on you—I almost believe it now. You make me laugh so hard that sometimes I can't breathe. You take too long to get ready, but I have to pretend I don't see everyone's eyes widen when you walk into a room. You carry yourself with such grace that I'm stuck wondering why in the world you would ever pick me.

You treat me like a queen, and in your eyes I deserve it, but I'm still waiting for my crown to fit.

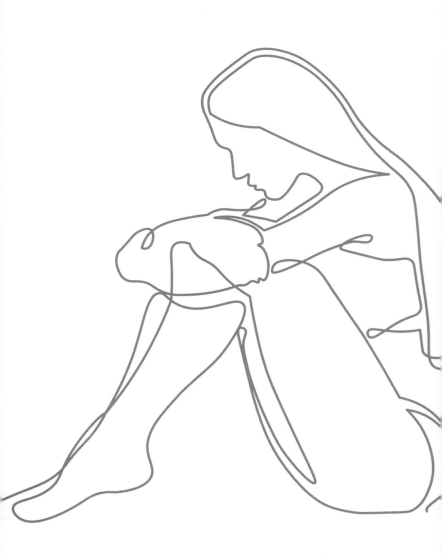

Things that guys do to give girls butterflies

1. When you two are talking, and he moves a piece of hair behind your ear—adorable.

2. If you're having a bad day and he asks, "What do you need? How can I help?"

3. He rubs your thumb while he is holding your hand.

4. When you walk into a room, he pats the seat he's saved for you.

5. When he asks, "When can I see you?"

6. He guides you through the crowd with his hand on your lower back.

How much is too much compromise?

No matter how much you love them, **remember that love does not mean you should tolerate anything less than you deserve**.

Compromise should be equal on both sides, not one person constantly having to bite their tongue to satisfy the other. Do not prioritize their happiness over your own. Acknowledge their feelings, but never allow them to make you feel like you have to give in if you want them to stay. The truth? If they were meant to stick around, they would empathize with your feelings too.

Don't ever confuse compromise with disrespecting yourself.

Live for you, not them.

SIGNS YOU'VE FOUND
a keeper

1 Their love feels unconditional. They've seen you at your best, and they've seen you at your worst, and they accept you for you.

2 They fight fair. There are bound to be disagreements, because not everyone is always 100 percent on the same page all of the time. However, you can talk about differences and work it out.

3 They're not just your partner, but they're truly your best friend.

How to deal
WHEN YOU HATE THEIR FRIENDS

It's weird when you love someone but dislike those they keep close. If you find yourself in that situation, try to keep these points in mind:

1. You are dating your partner, not their friends. You don't need to like them or even hang out with them. Each of you having your own friend group keeps a relationship healthy.

2. Your partner's friends have been around since before you were in the picture and might still be there if you ever break up. Remain respectful and civil and don't talk trash about them.

3. Unless a friend is a terrible influence, don't make your partner choose between them and you. You might lose.

Don't compare me to your ex

I don't want to hear that I'm better than them or how much you resent them. I don't want to feel hatred toward someone I've never even met and will never know like you did. I can't look at them through your eyes. They hurt you, but I'm not them. You loved them, but I love you now.

If comparing them to me makes you feel like you've made the right decision, I don't want to be a part of it.

My goal in being with you is to inspire you to grow, not be happy you left someone behind. If you're with me because I'm easier to be with than them, just know that is not enough for me.

I don't want
to make you

feel less for

someone else.

RELATIONSHIP
RED FLAGS

It's time to rethink a relationship when the other person:

Belittles your success.

Always second-guesses your decisions.

Gaslights you when you tell them how you feel.

Doesn't like it when you hang out with other people.

Makes you feel insecure about the relationship.

Is rarely there when you need them.

Annoys your family and friends.

Rarely apologizes, or when they do, it's just to end the argument.

Has no goals and constantly gets into trouble.

Never defends you when necessary.

Holds your past against you.

Is not supportive of changes that can make your life better.

Parties all of the time.

Never confronts you when you've done something wrong.

Makes you pay for everything.

Doesn't introduce you to their friends or family.

Consistently makes you feel anxious, not happy.

You weren't a maybe

You weren't just who I thought about when I wasn't thinking about someone else. You were the first person I messaged once I woke up in the morning and the last person I thought about before I went to bed. You were never one of many options. But I was the one you considered but never pursued. The one to raise your spirits when you needed it most. And the only one stupid enough to stick around when you chose her instead.

You weren't a maybe, but you are a never again.

You can't make someone love you by giving them more of what they already don't appreciate.

3 signs that she's losing interest

I find women often detach themselves emotionally before they detach themselves physically, so you could be losing her without even knowing it. Here are some signs she might be moving on:

She doesn't reply as often as she used to. Listen, everyone gets busy, but if she goes hours without talking or texting when you know she's not working, that's a sign.

She's not excited to tell you about her day. You ask, and you get a response like "Oh, it was good, how 'bout you?"

She doesn't make an effort to say good morning or good night to you anymore. That's a big one.

How to deal
when their friends don't like you

You want your partner's friends to like you. If they don't, it can feel detrimental to the relationship. However, it's not a deal-breaker. Here are five ways you can handle this situation.

1. Ask your partner if they know why their friends don't like you.

2. Let your partner know that it's disappointing; that you don't want to cause tension, but there is only so much you can do to fix it.

3. If it's something simple you can change, try to do it. But if it is out of your control, just let it go.

4. Be the bigger person, always. Be kind and respectful, even if they do not respond in kind. You are not the problem.

5. Keep conversations with them short and pleasant and avoid situations where you'll have to spend a ton of time together.

Avoiding jealousy

Jealousy comes in all different forms, from passive to possessive to angry. Regardless of the shape it takes, there are healthy ways to communicate envy.

Let's dissect this feeling.

Jealousy mainly occurs when you are feeling insecure about yourself or the relationship. Even if the feeling isn't based on fact but is just an inner demon whispering in your ear, you should never have to battle it alone. If you are overwhelmed with emotion, maybe talk with a friend before discussing it with your partner. Unless you have evidence otherwise, don't assume the worst, just **tell them how you are feeling.**.

While they may not respond the way you expect, if they listen and try to understand, that's the best you can hope for.

When you know it's over

We hate to admit that what once felt like a love story was just a fairy tale. You saw the red flags, and despite the disagreements, **you stayed**.

Suddenly, all the funny back-and-forths turned into real arguments that were never really resolved. You avoided conflict enough to "forget" it ever happened. Now you just act like everything is fine. The good morning and good night messages stop. "I'm sorry" doesn't seem to be a part of anyone's vocabulary. Your tears are no longer seen as a sign of real pain but as a reason to walk away.

Reassurance is nowhere to be found, only assumed. Time is made only to take naps in the middle of the day while keeping the phone on do not disturb. They see quotes you post to get their attention on your Instagram, but they don't care enough to ask what they mean. Someone asks how your relationship is, and you instantly get defensive. The person who used to hold you while you were upset

is now the person causing the breakdowns . . .
and you still think you two will last?

Love isn't reason enough to stay.

You can love someone and still be completely
wrong for each other. You can work on a
relationship and still fall short because you're the
only one trying. You may want to leave, but you
stay because you're comfortable and you feel
like they're all you know. Plus it's scary to start
over. You don't want to try to remember a new
person's favorite color, movie, snacks, and sports.
You don't want to meet someone else's family
and try to win over their siblings. You're tired,
and you just want to stick with what you
know. That's fine, **but are you happy?**
Until you make the break, you may
never know for sure.

**What is meant for you
will always find
its way to you.**

The recipe for us

You were perfect to me. You were the right amount of kind, the sweetest amount of consideration, topped perfectly with a pinch of sarcasm and sass. I craved you, your attention, your lust, your love, and your heart. I wouldn't change a single thing about you. I loved you for you.

Time went on, and I came to the realization that although there was nothing I wanted to change about you, there was one thing I wished I could change about myself—to be compatible with you. I tried everything I could: I poured in consideration and splashed in kindness, topped heavily with fun and attitude. **We just didn't blend together** as smoothly as I had thought. You were perfect. We weren't.

3 reasons he might give up

If he has to initiate everything—conversations, hangouts, whatever—and you never do, he will slowly get tired of trying.

If you don't allow him to find a balance between hanging out with the boys and hanging out with you, he might lose interest.

Guys rarely play hard to get, so if you think he's not interested, chances are he's not.

If one day we stop talking

I hope I'm someone you choose not to forget, that you think of me when you see a sunrise and smile knowing we used to enjoy them together. I hope you still watch our favorite TV shows and laugh at all the same scenes. I hope you reach your goals and silently thank me because **you know that I knew you could do it.** I even hope you love her better. I wasn't what you wanted, and I'm happy to have taught you that. Even though we decided to part ways,

I wish you everything I could never be for you.

RED FLAGS THAT THEY ARE
FURIOUS

1

When they are upset, and you try to hug them, they refuse to allow you to touch them.

2

They start laughing mid-argument, like they can't believe this is happening.

3

They say, "Do what you want," and then walk away. At that point, they are so mad they no longer want to argue.

Losing someone who wasn't really yours

You did it again. You cared too much and got attached. You read all the signs wrong, and now you're the one hurting. Is it even a heartbreak if they were never yours?

So maybe it wasn't official. Maybe you two never claimed to be significant others, but you still fell for them. You stayed up late talking. You spent endless hours thinking about them throughout your day. You memorized their favorite songs. You watched their favorite movies and shows. You learned how to play their favorite video game. You even started picking up on their gestures and expressions.

You loved them. You lost them. You're heartbroken. It's simple.

Don't ever think your feelings aren't valid, and don't think for a second that this loss is it for you. You may have lost someone who wasn't yours, but they lost someone who was willing to do anything to be theirs. **You're the prize.** You're the one that got away—not them. Enjoy this blessing in disguise.

You may not see it now, but one day the stars will align, the storm will settle, the wind will calm, and everything will fall into place. You'll understand then why things happened the way they did.

Just hold on.

Phases of a breakup

Phase 1: Denial

You think this break is temporary. You know what? Maybe it is. Every situation is different, but during this phase, please don't continually call them. Don't text them throughout the day. Give them their space. Let them miss you. Sometimes the more you try to persuade them to stay, the more they want to go. Take this time to focus on yourself. Give yourself the break you deserve. Hang out with your friends, catch up on your favorite shows, read the book you kept meaning to get to—do things that make **you** happy.

Phase 2: "I miss you"

So it is for real. They didn't come back. You're probably holed up in the comfiest spot in your room right now with no intention of getting up, and that's okay. Stay there for however long you want. Listen to sad songs, cry into your pillow, watch breakup movies, and dive deep into a TikTok hole. Go ahead and miss them unapologetically. There is just one thing I ask of you . . . please don't reach out to them. It's tempting, I know, but don't. Anything you need to tell them, write it down and put it in a jar or burn it. Nothing you say is going to change the way they feel. Please. *hugs*

Phase 3: Anger

You don't hate them. Okay, maybe a little, but you don't want to. You just wish they never existed, that you two never met, and that you didn't care so much. Why? Because if none of that had ever happened, then you wouldn't be sitting there hurting right now. I'm sorry that you feel so broken.

Phase 4: Acceptance

You're slowly letting go. You might still love them, and that's normal, but you don't long for them the way you did back when you were in phases 1 and 2. I am so proud of you. You see it now, right? The light at the end of the tunnel? It's still in the distance, but you know it's coming.

Phase 5: Repeat phases 2–4

This is where I'm sad to say that healing is never linear. You don't go through all the phases once and then call it a day. You go through these phases over and over again, still healing from the same heartbreak and wondering when the pain will end. I don't have an answer for you about how long it will take. Everyone heals at their own pace. Some people can move on within a couple of months, and for others, it takes years. There's no right or wrong time frame. Many people around you right now are silently healing from their own heartbreaks while still functioning. They are still doing their everyday tasks, making career moves, and acing exams. You can too. Although it hurts, please don't let the pain stop you from living your life. Please don't let this heartbreak consume you to the point that you lose yourself even more. There is so much beauty waiting for you at the end of the struggle. Please keep going.

Phase 6: Letting go and moving on

Congrats. You did it. You let them go and now you're moving on, but that's not why you should be proud of yourself.

You should be proud because
you did something you
thought you couldn't do.
You proved yourself wrong.

I don't think I'll ever get over you

As horrible as our relationship is now, I can't help but compare my future with our past.

I will never unsee the potential we had.

I will always think of you and wonder if this breakup was for the best, if leaving was truly the only option we had left. But we tried. We tried so hard for so long, and we both decided to end it before we resented each other. You will always be what I hoped for, but never what I really needed. And that's as close as I'll get to closure.

I admit I miss you

No one believed us when we said we were done.
I didn't either. I had thought this breakup would
make us fight for each other. But it just made us
realize how tired we were of fighting. How exhausted
we were from trying. How heartbreaking it was to
leave, but also how freeing it felt to let go. I'll admit
I miss you . . . but that's all.

You haven't
yet met all the
people who
are going to
love you.

Being too scared to love again

The more you understand love, the less you want to be in it. You realize that not everyone you love stays, and not every relationship lasts. Sometimes, they end before they even have a real chance to begin, and that's terrifying. Love comes with expectations, hope, and so much risk. You put your heart on the line, having faith that this person will take care of it.

After the relationship ends, the way you love each future person changes. You grow a little colder, you're a little less willing to compromise, and you just don't believe love alone is enough reason to stay. You're more hesitant to date seriously, and you start convincing yourself you don't need another person. Can I just say, you're right. **You don't need someone else**. You never did and you never will. However, if there is a day when someone fights to prove how willing they are to be that person for you, I hope you give them a chance. And just maybe, hopefully, they end up being the reason you believe in love all over again.

When you can't let someone go

If I ask you how they are, I bet you'll know the answer, even if you haven't talked to them in a while. You check their social media pages, you ask mutual friends, and maybe you even reach out because you are hoping to keep them in your life. I get it. It's nothing to be embarrassed about. **Letting someone go is not easy.**

You will have your good days and bad days. Some days you'll feel amazing and realize that everything happened for a reason, and then other days you'll just want to stay home, curl up in your blanket, listen to sad songs, and cry. It's okay.

It's okay to be sad. It's okay to miss them. It's okay if you're having a really hard time.

You can still love someone and never see them. You can still care and never talk. And you can let them go and miss them. Take your time letting them go. You don't have to be over them quickly, and you don't have to try to persuade yourself that you are. They came into your life, taught you things, were there for you when they could be, and now . . . well, now you have the opportunity to take all you've learned and start over again.

Go ahead and listen to the songs you loved, watch the show you two binge-watched, and look at all the pictures and videos. Just remember that it does get easier and, **as each day passes, you are proving just how strong you are.** You were okay before them, you'll be even better after them.

I'm rooting for you the same way you're rooting for them—from afar.

They found
someone new

It happened. You are casually scrolling through Instagram, and you have this urge to check up on them. You justify typing their name in the search bar by telling yourself it's been a while. That's when you stumble upon their newest post, the one that instantly makes your heart drop. All of a sudden you can't breathe. Who is this new person kissing the cheek of someone you once thought you were going to spend the rest of your life with? They are stunning. Their smiles are perfect. They look so happy together.

You start to wonder how your ex treats them. Do they get the flowers? They obviously get the Instagram "I love you" post. Do they get along with the family? Do they love watching *New Girl* together too? Do they pack your ex's lunch with cute little letters inside, wishing them a good day? Do they know how to calm them down when they're anxious? Can they make your ex's favorite soup when they're sick? Do they know your ex is terrified of commitment? Or are they the reason they got over that fear?

You want to know the answers to all these questions, but the only important question has already been answered: they are not the person for you.

Life works in
mysterious and
painful ways,
but things always
happen for
a reason.

Too little, too late

I can't undo the damage I have done. I ruined a good thing by letting my insecurities get in the way and by coping in the best way I know—by distancing myself, both emotionally and physically. My effort at the end was annoying because it should have been there since the beginning. I should have been there since day one. I take full responsibility for making you feel unwanted, for making you feel unloved, for hurting you to the point that you questioned whether or not you could ever open up to someone again. Nothing I say or do will ever make up for the hurt I've caused you. I pray that someone comes into your life who helps you believe that there are good people in this world. I may have learned from my mistakes a little too late, but you will always be my favorite "almost," my crushing "what if," and my biggest "I'm sorry."

I knew it was over the moment I realized you never asked about my day

I realized it when you were too busy to call or text me randomly just to check in. I realized it when I saw a couple laughing uncontrollably at a nearby table while we ate in silence and you stared at your phone. Don't get me wrong, I love you. I love you with every fiber of my being. I would have dedicated my life to you, but we knew it was over when we realized we were no longer happy. Making time for each other was no longer a reward, but a chore. Compromising turned into giving up the fight just to get by.

We were great until we weren't, and that's okay.

I wanted it to be you

You were supposed to return from work as I was setting the table for spaghetti night. Our son would rush up and give you the biggest hug. You'd swoop him up in your arms and tickle him, while walking over to give me my "I'm home" kiss. Our baby girl would be sitting in her high chair smiling now that you were back.

That's all I wanted. **That's all we wanted.** Now? Now I just want to finish listening to a song without crumbling. I want to grab food without knowing what you'd order on the menu. I want to sleep without waking up crying because you were in my dreams. I want to erase all the good memories and only remember the bad to remind myself why we didn't work out in the first place. I wanted it to work out. I wanted it to be you.

When they decide to love again, they love hard—but it takes patience.

They don't fall easily—it takes more than just good conversation, attraction, and things in common to win them over.

HOW TO SPOT THE
brokenhearted

They can come off as cold. If they see one red flag, they're over it.

As soon as they notice someone they care about is changing up on them, they don't even hesitate, they walk away. They do not want to go through that pain again.

Right now,
you are
finally focused
on yourself.

Is it really over?

Letting someone go is difficult, but it's even harder when you can't stop thinking "what if?" What if they change their mind? What if they come back to me? What if this was all one huge misunderstanding and we will be together soon? What if?

Listen, I don't know who needs to hear this, but I'm going to say it anyway—if they wanted to, they would. **If they wanted to be with you, they would.** If they wanted you back, they would reach out. Or better yet, if they wanted it to work out, they would never have walked away in the first place. If they wanted to fight for you, they would have. And you wouldn't be stuck here with the what ifs.

Instead, you are blessed with the right nows. Right now, you are on your way to moving on and letting go. Right now, you are doing what makes you happy. **Right now, you are on your way to okay,** and you will soon be fine. This feeling of heartbreak and devastation is just . . . right now.

A few things that can help you get over a breakup

- Cut off all communication. I know that sounds really hard, because it is. But it only takes a few weeks to create a new habit, and you need to get into the habit of not having them in your life.

- Change up your environment, whether it is cleaning out your room or changing your perfume, as scent carries memories.

- Listen to sad music and let your feelings out. Scream, cry, bawl your eyes out—allow yourself to feel the pain of the loss.

- Write a list of reasons why this breakup happened and read it over whenever you think about reaching out to them.

The next

I still remember the way you smell. I could probably draw your smile from memory. I can still pick out your laugh in a crowd of people. I can recite our last conversation because I've replayed it in my mind so many times. I still love you. I think I always will.

But I can't bring myself to start over, because I know how it ends. I know that no matter how much we try, it will never work. Maybe, just maybe, knowing this can be enough to try to move on—knowing that I can't go backward, that my only choice is to hope I can love someone else one day.

Will I ever love them the same way I loved you? No. But that's okay. You will always be a part of me. I can make new memories and still cherish the old ones. You can too.

Can we be friends?

Sometimes I wish we had just stayed friends.
Sometimes I wish we hadn't taken that leap of faith
and believed in love, that we just left our friendship
alone, because now I have to get used to a life
without you. Now I have to adapt to this new world
of meeting people and going through things without
you behind me, assuring me everything is going to
be fine. But we can't be friends now. The love we
had makes seeing you either painful or just weird,
because how are we supposed to act now?

When I
lost you . . .

. . . I also lost
my best friend.

FRIENDSHIP
FRIENDSHIP
FRIENDSHIP
FRIENDSHIP

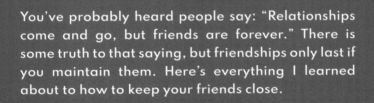

You've probably heard people say: "Relationships come and go, but friends are forever." There is some truth to that saying, but friendships only last if you maintain them. Here's everything I learned about to how to keep your friends close.

Starting a friendship

The best relationships come naturally, where you gain a connection without even trying. It's easy to make time for each other because you both enjoy the company. Plus, maybe it's just convenient—you see them all the time in passing, you have a mutual friend, or they share an interest with you. But turning a casual hang into a friendship is an effort, when you realize, "Wow, I want to have this beautiful soul in my life." As scary as it is to try, you never know how important they may become in the months and years to come.

You may be one "hello" away from a friendship you never knew you needed.

hello

5 ways to maintain a friendship

1. Understand that you each have your own lives and you don't need to be together all day, every day.

2. Just because you are friends doesn't mean you have to agree with everything they say or believe—agree to disagree and respect your differences.

3. Prioritize hangouts with them and put dates on the calendar.

4. Check up on them even when they aren't in crisis.

5. Be supportive of their goals, dreams, and ambitions.

Finding your home

Change is growth, and with growth comes the fear of new beginnings. Is that fear stopping you? Are you settling where you're comfortable, but underestimating your ability to flourish and thrive elsewhere? Only leaving when you are no longer wanted or needed, but if given the opportunity to stay, you would, because it's what you know?

Maybe one day you'll stumble upon a new beginning, maybe a friendship, that's warm and welcoming. **You experience a different kind of comfortable.** Try to remember that change may lead to the people who can make you feel like you're home.

I never looked at you and saw my best friend—that title isn't enough. You are my comfort, my twin flame, my sanctuary.

It's not a competition

When something good happens, the only thing better is telling a good friend your news. I like the saying, **"A win for you is a win for them, and a win for them is a win for you. Why? Because you two are on the same team."**

A real friend will never envy your success. A real friend will never make you feel bad for wanting to celebrate your achievements. A real friend will never consider you to be competition. It shouldn't even cross their mind, and if it does—they're not a real friend.

A few ways
to be there
for your friend
in a crisis

- Give them your undivided attention.

- Realize that sometimes all you have to do is listen.

- Understand their feelings, don't invalidate them.

- Let them figure out the solution to their situation on their own, but provide input and opinions if they ask.

- Reassure them that they will not go through it alone.

- If they aren't ready or can no longer talk about it, provide their favorite snacks and watch their comfort show or movie with them. Sometimes just physically being there is enough.

Cherish the good ones

We cycle through friends all the time—one year you're really close to someone, and then the next you two barely even talk. However, if you're lucky enough to meet someone who tries hard to be consistent in your life, cherish them. You can call randomly, and they'll pick up the conversation as if you two never stopped talking. If your car breaks down, they'll be there in a heartbeat with jumper cables.

But a true friend is not a "yes" man or woman. They don't just agree with you all the time. They tell you the harsh truth when you need to hear it. They know how to balance empathy with honesty and come at it with pure intentions. They are considerate of your feelings, but also well aware of when you are at your limit. They understand your silences and blank stares. They are rooting for you all the time. They will become the standard for all your future friendships, but **few ever measure up.**

Sometimes I want to talk about my problems and just have you listen, not try to fix anything or say what you would do.

Just listen.

Thank you to my best friend

To the person who recognizes exactly what I'm thinking just by the expression on my face.

Who knows what to say and do when I feel like my world is falling apart.

Who is willing to listen to me rant about the same situation over and over until I'm spent.

Who won't judge me, no matter what I say, but who cares enough to tell me when I'm in the wrong.

To the person who unintentionally saved me— I wouldn't be me without you.

You aren't best friends unless . . .

- You have inside jokes that no one else understands.

- **You dislike many of the same people.**

- You understand everything they're saying just with facial expressions.

- **You know when they are lying.**

- When you met, you weren't sure if you were going to like each other.

- **Sitting in silence is comfortable.**

- Your house is their house.

- **When one of you is going through something, both of you are going through it.**

- You didn't realize how awfully your ex-best friends treated you until you met your current best friend, who treats you beautifully.

THREE WAYS YOU KNOW YOU'RE BEST FRIENDS

1

It's a bad idea but then you look at each other like, "I'll do it if you do it."

2

You are occasionally mean to each other and don't take it personally.

3

Your parents love them but they also know that if you two are together, crazy things are going to happen.

127

Difficult conversations in friendships

Friends are there to support you, to build you up when you are down, and to remind you that no matter what happens, you will never struggle alone. However, friendships are not always rainbows and sunshine. A good friend wants what is best for you, which means they will call you out when you are wrong or are making poor choices. But who wants to hear that, especially from someone who's supposed to be in your corner? Sometimes even having these conversations can make or break the friendship.

But before you walk away angry, remember that these talks come with pure intentions. Your friend loves you, which is why they are willing to put a friendship on the line to tell you the truth. **Try to take the advice in the spirit that it's given.** You need friends who are willing to have these talks with you. Otherwise, are they really your friend?

Ways to maintain friendships when you're in love

New love is exciting, but don't get so swept up that you forget about the other people in your life. Here are a few tips to keep your close friends close:

- Plan hangs for just the two of you.

- When you are together, focus on catching up with them—put the phone away.

- Check up on them with calls or text messages, especially on important days for them.

- Let them know when you miss them or are thinking about them.

- While you're happy about your romantic relationship, try to talk about other things as well.

- Avoid canceling on your friends just because your significant other is free.

- Provide opportunities for your friend and your romantic partner to get to know each other, but don't push them into being friends.

Dealing with friend jealousy

Friend jealousy, while common, is the worst. It comes in many forms, including feeling left out when your friend hangs out with other people, or talks too much about another friend, or never seems to have time for you anymore. Keep in mind that while friendship is a beautiful support system, one relationship should not make or break your life.

However, if your best friend's other relationships make you feel insecure, acknowledge that.

If you feel it is impacting your relationship, mention it to your friend. Hopefully, they can reassure you that, regardless of the other people in their life, they'll always be your friend as well.

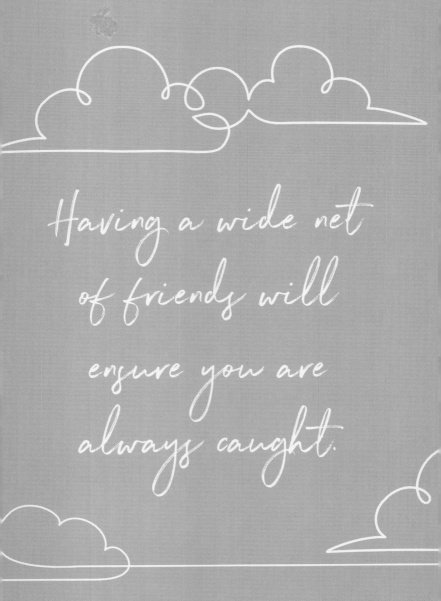

Having a wide net
of friends will

ensure you are

always caught.

Long-distance friendships

My best friendships tend to be low maintenance: the ones where you two don't **have** to talk every single day, the ones where you don't get upset if the other person has a busy schedule. I think of them as healthy friendships with healthy boundaries. However, long-distance friendships add a level of difficulty because, for the most part, they occur through calls, messaging, and social media. This means it can take more effort to have a true emotional understanding of the other person. I'm not saying long-distance friendships are bad, just that they're harder—but some people are worth it, especially when it is the only way you can keep them in your life.

Here are some options for easy maintenance:

1. Text and call them when you have time, but don't expect an immediate answer.

2. Schedule regular FaceTime dates to ensure periodic catch-ups.

3. Check in more often if they are going through difficult times, even if it is just a "how are you doing today?" text.

4. Send them random memes or videos just so they know you're thinking of them.

5. Let them know when you are busy or will be delayed in responding.

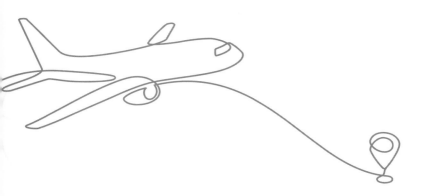

HOW TO APOLOGIZE

AND MEAN IT

Saying a sincere sorry can be difficult because
you have to take responsibility for hurting another
person. If you have a hard time apologizing,
here are some steps that can help.

1

Are you actually
sorry? Be sure.
If not, come back
when you are
truly ready to
make amends.

2

Begin by
expressing
remorse for
hurting them.

3

Remind them that
your relationship is
way more important
than whatever you
are arguing about.

4

Next, reiterate their feelings. Explaining why you think they are upset in your own words can be an opportunity to make sure you understand how they feel and what you did wrong. That way you both are clear about why you are apologizing. It also aids in validating their feelings and making your apology feel more genuine.

Even then, there's no way to be sure that the person will forgive you. But if you've sincerely tried to make amends, you've done all you can do.

5

6

Express remorse again and explain that you are ready to compromise and/ or to never offend or hurt them in the same way again.

Growing apart

One universal truth is that time does not stop for anyone. We get older, grow wiser, and lose people who don't change as we do. Sadly, some of those people are ones we mistakenly thought were going to be in our lives forever.

Sometimes it's not something that happened, but what didn't happen. You two stopped talking, stopped catching up, until you have no idea what is going on in each other's lives. You two connected because your environment allowed and supported it. But now that you both are into different things, going to new schools, starting new jobs, meeting new people, you realize it's either time to put in that extra effort to see each other or move on. Either way, that's okay.

Part of growing up is letting go.

What to keep in mind when you and your friend are arguing

Disagreements in friendships can be emotionally draining. Regardless of the outcome, fights are scary, because there's always a chance a fight could end the friendship. Here are a couple of things to keep in mind:

- Is what you're arguing about worth the fight? Or could you agree to disagree?

- Try to keep calm and lay all the cards on the table with an open mind.

- Are both parties at least trying to understand the other person's feelings?

- Listen and take a breath before responding, so you don't blurt out something you may regret.

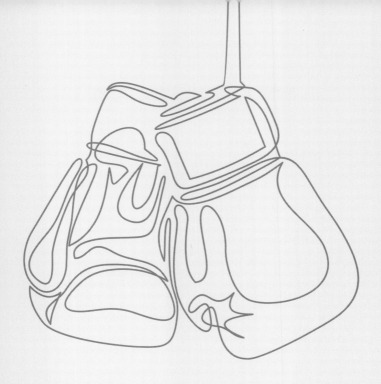

- Avoid involving other people in the argument—this is between the two of you.

- Once you've heard both sides, really think about whether or not it is something you two can work through.

- Compromising is an option, but never compromise your self-respect to keep anyone in your life.

Friendship red flags

- They don't prioritize hanging out or always cancel at the last minute.

- They "tease" you to entertain others and get irritated that you don't think it is funny.

- They never reach out to you, and if they do, it's only because they need something.

- They can't give you a compliment without insulting you a little at the same time.

- They say you are overreacting when you tell them how you feel.

- They are constantly competing with you, even though you should be on the same team.

- They aren't happy when you succeed.

- They don't like it when you have other friends.

- They make you feel insecure about your choices.

- They make you feel bad for having feelings.

- They haven't got your back.

- They don't want you to change or grow.

- They don't tell you when they are mad; they just silently hold a grudge.

According to you, I'm doing well. But that's because you don't really want to know. You're never around long enough to see me cry.

Farewell, friend

I have always understood that not everyone stays in your life forever. I know that everything happens for a reason, people leave for a reason . . . I just never expected you to be one of them. We were inseparable. Regardless of what was going on in my life, you were the light at the end of the tunnel.

You gave me hope. You gave me reason to believe that no matter how I struggled, you would be right there with me. You knew me better than anyone else. You saw sides of me I have never shown to others. This has to be the hardest goodbye yet.

Not everyone stays in your life forever, but I wish you had.

Ways to deal with losing a friend

While it is natural that friends become closer or more distant over time, it doesn't mean losing someone you love is easy. Here are a few ideas to help you get through it:

- If your friend has dropped out of your life without telling you why, maybe ask for a reason. It could have been caused by something you did or said, but it also could be something they are going through on their own, like depression. It's not always you.

- If you can't talk to them, write them a letter, pouring out all of your feelings on paper. You don't have to send it, but it might help you get closure.

- While your mind is in overdrive, don't forget to care for your body. Drink water, get outside, eat healthy food, and try to sleep. It won't help the pain in your heart, but it will make it easier to heal.

History means nothing

Sometimes old friends become a burden. We keep hanging out with them because we always have, even when they no longer make us happy or they even make us feel bad. I'm sure you've thought this, but I'm going to say it anyway: knowing someone for a long time is not a reason to allow them to treat you poorly. If anything, they should know better. They should understand you more. They should know where your boundaries lie.

The more you defend the friendship with your shared history, the more you're disrespecting yourself.

Harsh, I know, but I'm sure you've thought it—I just wrote it.

HOW TO LEAVE A FRIENDSHIP

Your friends help shape you as a person. Someone who might be great for you at one time in your life may grow into someone who is holding you back or bringing out the worst in you. But leaving a friendship is difficult and uncomfortable to do. If you do end up making the break to help better yourself as a person, I'm proud of you. Here are some ways to leave on good terms:

1. Decide whether or not you can let the friendship fade naturally or you need to actually give them a reason why you don't want to be friends anymore.

2. If it is the latter, keep the focus on your decision, not their behavior. Let them know that although you appreciated having them in your life, you need time to focus on yourself now, so they will be seeing you less often.

3. Keep it civil, and avoid talking about them to other people. For example, turn down their offers to hang out, but thank them for the invite anyway.

4. Through it all, remember that your emotional well-being is the priority. Outside of being kind when you can, you don't have to explain yourself or justify your actions.

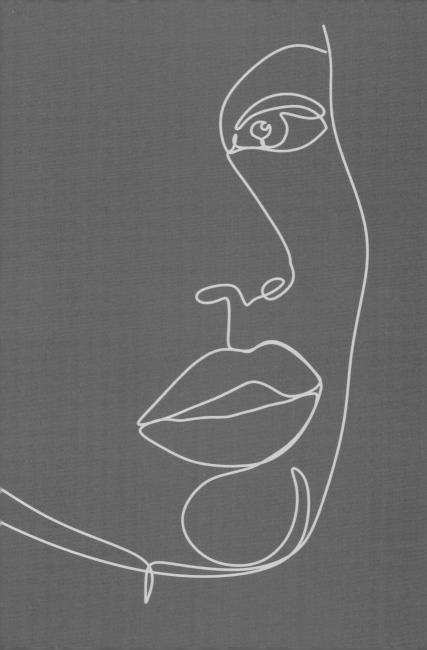

SELF
SELF
SELF
SELF

The relationships you have with others reflect the relationship you have with yourself. Do you love you the way they do?

Are you overthinking?

It's okay to go through every possible scenario in your head to determine the best way to move forward. It's okay to worry and hope that things will work out for the best.

However, it is not okay to allow these thoughts to consume you.

Your brain is a powerful tool, but your thoughts are not facts and do not determine who you are as a person. Our heads can trick us to believe every horrible thought is true.

WHEN YOU ARE OVERTHINKING,  ASK  YOURSELF THIS QUESTION:

Are these your feelings and thoughts, or are they just a reflection of your worst fear?

Bad day silver lining

Some days just don't go as hoped. Sometimes you wake up and have to debate whether or not it's even worth getting up. While your to-do list is long, it's still not reason enough to get moving. When you finally drag yourself out of bed, every little thing irritates you. There's nothing that could make this day better except for it to end.

But maybe we shouldn't curse the bad days. Sometimes they are necessary in order to appreciate what's to come. Everyone wants sunshine, but how would you know if you didn't have rain? Try to think of it as a blessing in disguise.

3 a.m. thoughts

It's easy to avoid feelings when I'm surrounded by people. All day I overstimulate my mind and congest my schedule, drowning out my worries. It's nights like these when I'm forced to sit with my thoughts, my regret, and my own disappointment, when I'm forced to face myself. It's nights like these when my pillow is soaked with tears that I realize, "Wow. I'm not okay."

Late at night, my anxiety starts to consume me, and I have nothing but music to help ease my mind. The truth? In the light of day, I know everything will eventually fall into place. I know that all the obstacles I'm experiencing will help me grow as a person, and that even if I got everything I wanted, these feelings would still exist. But at 3 a.m., the darkness of the sky unleashes the worst feelings I have buried deep within my heart.

Spiraling through the good, the bad, the impossible, I wonder—do my friends know? Am I transparent enough for them to see I am struggling internally? Or do they just see the smiles, hear my laughter, and trust I'd tell them if anything were wrong?

I know I will wake up tomorrow and conquer another day, even with these thoughts eating me alive at night. And maybe, just maybe, I will open up and tell someone I love. Why? Because they deserve the truth, and I deserve the help.

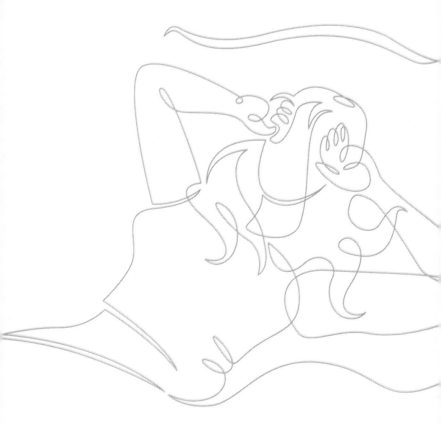

Am I the problem?

Maybe people have a mistaken perception of you that you can't change. Whether it is true or not, you will have to accept that they believe you are part of the reason they are miserable.

Does this mean you are the problem? Maybe—no one is perfect.

But just because people in your life have their reasons doesn't mean they are right.

Similarly, how you see others doesn't necessarily mean they are the problem. Try to keep this in mind instead of continually blaming yourself or trying to change someone's opinion of you.

No matter how "good"
you think you are,
you are bound to
be the villain in
someone else's story.

I may be down.
I may be sad.
I may be
frustrated.

But that
never stopped
me before and
it never will.

It's okay to not be okay

I don't know who needs to hear this, but it's okay to not be okay, Most important, it's okay to not be okay and not have a reason or a way to explain why you're feeling the way you're feeling. So many people assume there has to be a cause. Sometimes there is no reason and no way to explain it.

You feel how you feel, and that's okay.

Don't be afraid to ask for help

"I'll deal with this later."

"Out of sight, out of mind."

"It'll pass."

Okay, so you don't want to deal with what's wrong, or you don't know how to. You cope by avoiding emotions and acting like they don't exist, hoping they go away. But you're tired of feeling the way you're feeling.

Sometimes there is no real explanation for your feelings, but the lack of explanation does not invalidate the emotions. Holding on to this emotional pressure and living on autopilot is not healthy. Asking for help is not a cry for attention. Seeking a solution to the knots you feel in your heart and mind is not pointless nor a waste of time.

Your mental health is not a waste of time. Use this turmoil as the gateway to accepting the help you deserve.

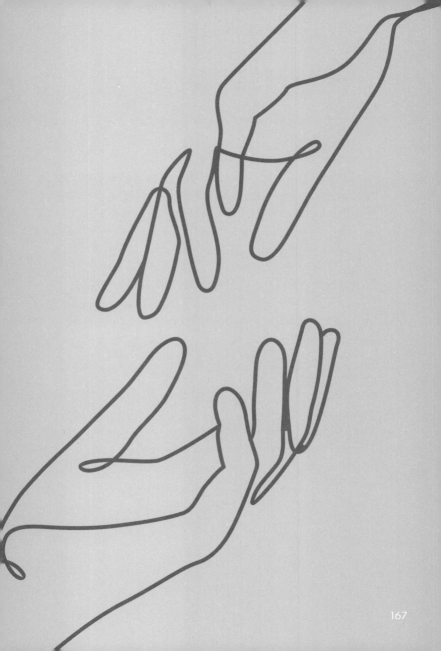

Prioritizing self-care

Sometimes you spend your days worrying so much about everyone else and making sure they're okay that taking a minute for yourself seems impossible or feels selfish. But I'm here to tell you it's not—it's essential. Ask yourself: How are you today? How are you feeling? How are you coping with everything going on in your life? Are you okay? **Because you matter too.** Taking care of those you love is important, but taking care of yourself should be your top priority.

Are you happy? Because you deserve to be happy too. Do something for you today. Play video games, go to the gym, stay in bed and watch your favorite movie, have a bowl of ice cream, or escape with a book. They say that those who hurt in private heal in silence, but I hear your silence. If someone hasn't told you this yet today, I'm proud of you for making yourself a priority.

169

4 ways to start loving yourself more

1. Stop comparing your life to others. What you see is just a sliver of their reality, so it's not even fair to judge. Focus instead on you and what you want out of life.

2. Realize everyone has an opinion, but that doesn't make it a fact. You are not going to please everyone, so just learn to please yourself.

3. Remember that how your body looks is not who you are as a person.

4. Don't label feelings "good" or "bad"— accept that all are a part of life and try to feel them.

I guess I never looked for the light at the end of the tunnel. I just kept moving forward, head down, and trusted myself to get there, someday, somehow.

Forgive yourself

The best people in your life probably weren't born that way. In order to be so understanding and kind, they probably made mistakes or were bullied and misjudged. They've probably gone through periods of being bitter and angry as well—no one is perfect.

But it's hard to become a better person if you don't grow and learn from your past mistakes.

I understand that learning to move on from the past is difficult, especially if you are ashamed or embarrassed about your behavior. I know what it's like to think back and just crumble because the person you are now would never make those horrible, impulsive decisions. But you need to forgive yourself. Why? Because if you don't, you are punishing yourself for something that eventually made you a better person.

I haven't figured out everything . . .

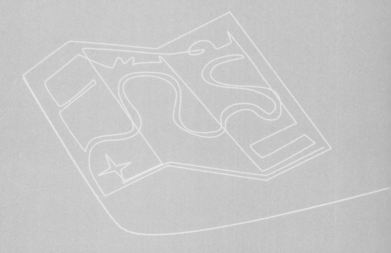

. . . yet.

Why do I feel so lonely?

Have you ever been at a party or with a group of people and just felt a wave of loneliness? You are talking and smiling and surrounded by people, but you feel like you could disappear and no one would really care?

While I sometimes enjoy a crowd, I believe in quality over quantity. If you can have one or two people you consider close, the rest don't matter. The truth is, sometimes, even with both—quality and quantity—life can feel lonely and like no one understands you, but **realize you have people that are willing to try.**

Monitoring your social battery

Going out to be with your friends can be fun, but a quick reminder: you're not obligated to go. When a get-together feels overwhelming, you need to be clear about your boundaries. You also don't always have to explain why you don't want to go out—**it's healthy to have some time for yourself to recharge.** Your real friends will understand.

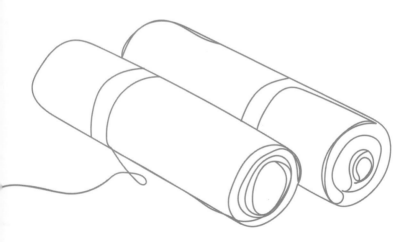

WHEN ANXIETY TAKES OVER

You don't have to be okay right away, and you don't have to try to hide it.

I don't think all people truly understand how heavy the world can feel when you're overwhelmed with anxiety, but I do. Your feelings are valid. Be aware of whatever triggered this heaviness and try to understand it. Take some time to breathe, listen to soothing music, monitor your heart rate, and let's explore how you feel.

- Is the cause something that can be fixed?

- Is this something that will just pass without your reacting?

- Is a reaction necessary? If so, are there any small steps you can take toward addressing it?

- Does anyone else know how you're feeling? If not, will saying how you feel out loud make you feel better?

- Could it be physical? Have you eaten something healthy and did you drink enough water today? Did you sleep last night?

If what's triggering your anxiety is not something you can fix or change, you need to start to accept the feeling and try to move forward. You know yourself best—what is your next move? Maybe go for a walk in the woods, talk with a trusted friend, or burn it off dancing to your favorite song. But try to remember that these feelings are temporary, and they will pass.

The truth about quiet people

- Once they are comfortable with you, they will talk a lot.

- They are the best listeners.

- They are very observant, so they see everything and notice energy shifts.

- The inside of their head can be noisy with thoughts.

- If they make the first move, it's going to be through social media or text.

- They are the last people to ask for help.

- They tend to have more self-awareness.

Three things people do
when they don't want to admit they're sad

1

They use music as therapy— headphones always in, ignoring everything else.

3

They distract themselves with their hobbies, whether it is the gym or gaming or baking.

2

They let it out at night, when the emotions start to get to them, but are buttoned up in the morning as if nothing happened.

Dealing with insecurities

We've all heard that a picture is worth a thousand words, but often those words aren't kind. We all want to look good in every photo, but we are our own harshest critics. For every photo posted online, there were hundreds of attempts that didn't make the cut. Even when we are finally satisfied, we still feel the need to trick the viewer's eye. Waist isn't small enough? Photoshop. Have a breakout? Facetune. Technology has made it so easy for us to fool everyone else into thinking that perfection isn't out of reach, when in the end we are only fooling ourselves into thinking that what we have to offer will never be beautiful enough to really share.

Have you ever tried to take a photo of a gorgeous sunset? When you are in the moment, it's absolutely breathtaking. You take a picture with your phone and it looks all right, maybe a little blurry. But no matter how much you tweak it, **the photo will never capture the moment's beauty in real life.** Read that again, because the same is true for you.

Other people's opinions

I like all kinds of ice cream, but I prefer chocolate. That doesn't mean vanilla isn't delicious, I just like the flavor of chocolate better. You may feel different, and that's okay. **Someone else's opinion or preference doesn't devalue yours**—it's not a fact or even necessarily based in truth. The same is true about their opinion of you.

If you need outside reassurance from other people, go to someone you trust. There are probably only four or five people's opinions that actually matter in your life. Think about who they are and seek them out. Nobody else matters.

Being enough

Everyone makes it seem like being with someone is so important, that having a relationship somehow means you are "ahead" in life. You may not have your career down, but hey, you have a boyfriend or girlfriend, so all is good, right?

But don't you also know people who are not in a relationship, who fly freely through life enjoying things that matter, like school, work, family, and friends? Maybe they've decided that they aren't going to chase the attention of someone who might like them someday and instead focus on what makes them happy now.

They are nurturing what they love about themselves, rather than seeking approval from the outside.

You don't need validation from other people. The only person you should aim to be enough for is yourself.

Value you.
Love you,
exactly as
you are.

THINGS I'M STILL TRYING TO LEARN

While I've written a whole book about emotions and relationships, I've still got a lot to learn, including:

1

I can't be everything to everyone.

2

The numbers on the scale don't define me.

3

Some things are better left unsaid.

4

I can't overwork myself to avoid my feelings.

6

I need to let
people be there
for me the
way I'm there
for them.

5

You can still be
nice and tell
people no.

7

Avoiding
someone to push
them away is not
how you say
goodbye.

8

Not everyone
deserves my
energy.

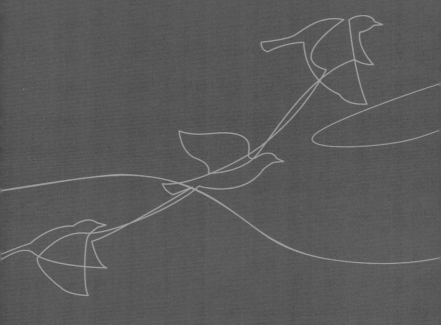

CONCLUSION CONCLUSION CONCLUSION CONCLUSION

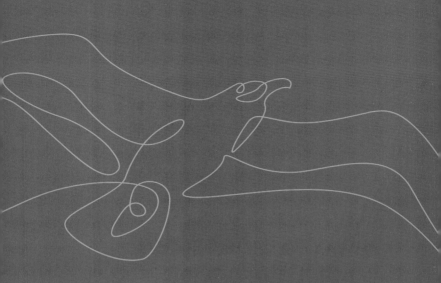

In my life, I have had the pleasure of being surrounded by and learning from wonderful people with beautiful souls. I have also had the honor of interacting with amazing supporters on social media who just want to feel understood and heard. Well, I've heard you, I've seen you, I'm with you. This book is for you. And maybe it's not about finding your person.

Maybe it's realizing, understanding, and accepting that your person has been you all along . . . and you are more than enough . . . you always have been.

About the author

Growing up in the San Francisco Bay Area as a first-generation Filipino American, Anne was a sounding board for friends and family. When she graduated from college and began teaching, her students looked to her for encouragement as well. So when she joined TikTok in 2019, it was natural for her to start posting about relationships. Anne's first advice post grew out of watching a girl failing to get a guy's attention at the gym. Since then, Anne's relationship posts have helped her social media to grow to millions of followers on TikTok, Instagram, and YouTube.

Credits

Illustrations of Anne by Victoria Rusyn, 10 and 190

Shutterstock.com 4691, 104; Alex_l, 49; alla_line, 52, 98; art of line, 22; asesidea, 164; Back one line, 134, 135; bintankmedia, 2, 3, cover; Blinx, 35; Borisovna.art, 30, 31, 127, 136, 137; Brasova Hanna, 55; Buntoon Rodseng, 28; Buryi Bogdan, 89; Daiquiri, 167; Dasha D, 5, 8, 9; Derplan13, 161; Dychkova Natalya, 110, 111, 171, 186, 187; Inna Rogach, 79; IrAnat, 147: juliawhite, 175; JustArtNina, 41; Kamila Bay, 165; Kraska, 116; LivDeco, 61; LuckyStep, 158; Magic Panda, 112, 113; Mitoria, 95; MP2021, 67; Muhammad Muammar, 73; nasharaga, 62; Nataletado, 156; Natalllenka.m, 183; NikVector, 141; Olga Rai, 154, 155; OliaGraphics, 61; Olya_molli, 47; OneLineStock.com, 24, 32, 33, 86, 150, 186, 187; Pavlo S, 14, 107; Plasteed, 58; pimchawee, 97; Rusyn, 20, 39, 69, 169; samui, 81; Seiraa Art, 176; Sell Vector, 72, 124, 125, 141; Simple Line, 92, 93, 120, 174; Singleline, 12, 37, 85, 91, 103, 114, 139, 148, 152, 192; StocKNick, 19; suginami 129; Tanya Syrytsyna, 133; tetiana_u, 158; Valenty, 34, 43, 46; Venko Vika, 170; Walnut Bird, 50, 51, 130, 131; Yanina Nosova, 177; YuliiaOsadcha, 121; ZABIIAKA Oleksandr, 119